Did you know that golf balls were once made of wood? Or that in the early days of baseball, it took *four* strikes to make an out? Would it surprise you to learn that bowling began as a religious ceremony? The history of sport is filled with fascinating facts, some of which you can read about in this book.

CONTENTS

Table Tennis (Ping-Pong)   **5**
Bowling   **8**
Boxing   **14**
Golf   **21**
Baseball   **27**
Skiing   **32**
Badminton   **40**

*Text copyright © 1980 by Don L. Wulffson
Illustrations copyright © 1980 by Roy Doty
All rights reserved. No part of this book may be reproduced or
utilized in any form or by any means, electronic or mechani-
cal, including photocopying, recording or by any information
storage and retrieval system, without permission in writing
from the Publisher. Inquiries should be addressed to Lothrop,
Lee & Shepard Books, a division of William Morrow &
Company, Inc., 105 Madison Avenue, New York, N.Y. 10016.
Printed in the United States of America.
First Edition
1 2 3 4 5 6 7 8 9 10*

*Library of Congress Cataloging in Publication Data
Wulffson, Don L
   How sports came to be.
   SUMMARY: Relates the origins of table tennis, bowling,
boxing, baseball, badminton, skiing, and golf.
   1. Sports—History—Juvenile literature.   [1. Sports—History]
I. Doty, Roy, (date)   II. Title.
GV571.W84   796'.09   79-26237
ISBN 0-688-41924-0   ISBN 0-688-51924-5 lib. bdg.*

HOW SPORTS CAME TO BE

DON L. WULFFSON

Illustrated by
Roy Doty

Lothrop, Lee & Shepard Books
New York

TABLE TENNIS (PING-PONG)

Table tennis was invented in England during the nineteenth century. All the equipment used in those early days was homemade. The ball was made of string. Books put down the middle of a table made the first net. The paddle was cut out of a piece of thick cardboard.

Balls of rubber or cork soon replaced balls made of string. Some balls were covered with a knitted web or a piece of cloth to give them more spin.

The balls we use today were originally children's toys. A man named James Gribb noticed children playing with the hollow celluloid balls. He tried them out at table tennis and discovered that they were perfectly suited to the game.

The first real ping-pong paddles looked like little drums. They had very long handles and hollow blades covered with leather.

Next, wooden paddles shaped like the ones we use today were invented. But the surface of the paddles was too slick. It did not give the player enough control.

One day a man named E.C. Goode was in a drugstore searching for a remedy for a headache. He noticed a studded rubber cash mat on the counter. The thought came to him that it would make a good surface for a ping-pong paddle. His headache forgotten, Goode bought the mat. He took it home, cut it down to the right size, and glued it to the paddle.

The new paddle gave Goode a great deal more control over the ball. It improved his game so much that he challenged the British national champion. Goode won, fifty games to three!

BOWLING

Bowling is at least 7,000 years old. It is one of the oldest of all sports. Stone Age people, the ancient Egyptians, and the early inhabitants of the South Sea Islands all played forms of the game.

It may seem hard to believe, but modern bowling got its start as part of Christian religious ceremonies. Inside the church a wooden pin was set up. The pin represented the devil. One after another, churchgoers would roll or throw a ball at the pin. Being able to knock down the pin was like being able to knock down the devil.

After a while people began to like bowling for its own sake. Soon what had been a religious ceremony became a popular sport.

In the early days of the sport the ball was a large, round stone. Then came wooden balls. Later, iron and then rubber balls were tried.

STONE   WOODEN   IRON   RUBBER

WOODEN   MODERN

For a long time the balls had to be palmed—that is, rolled off the end of the hand. Then came the idea of drilling finger holes into the ball. At first just two holes were drilled, one for the thumb and one for the middle finger. Then came the three-hole ball, which is the most popular type today.

In the early days of the game, each player brought his own pin. As many pins were used as there were players. In time, the number of pins was set at nine. The game of "ninepins" became popular in Europe and America.

In America, ninepins became a gambling game. It was played in places where thieves and crooks hung out. Because of this, ninepins was outlawed. To get around the law, one more pin was added. And because the law said that "ninepins" was illegal but didn't say anything about "tenpins," there was nothing the police could do.

And that is why to this day the game of bowling is played with ten pins.

BOXING

Boxing has been popular since the earliest beginnings of civilization. Pictures at least 7,000 years old show men boxing with their hands wrapped with some sort of material. People in some primitive tribes are known to have fought with their hands protected by thick pads of string. Some island people turned their fists into deadly weapons by arming them with rows of shark teeth.

In earliest times, boxing knew no rules, ring, or rounds. A fight ended only when one of the boxers lay beaten and bleeding.

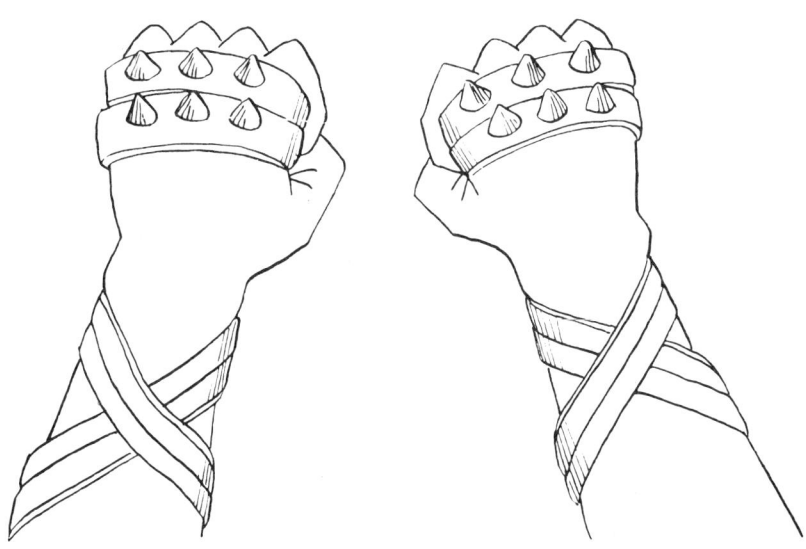

Boxing was an important sport in the early days of Rome and Greece. Until 400 B.C., fighters wound soft strips of leather around their hands and arms. Then came gloves of hardened leather, which, in many ways, were like brass knuckles. Then came an even uglier and more dangerous invention–the Roman *cestus*. The cestus was a leather hand-covering studded with sharp little metal nuggets.

Fights in those days were often to the death.

Boxing had become too cruel and bloody, and the "sport" almost disappeared for several hundred years. Not until the seventeenth century did it make a comeback, in England.

But boxing still remained a very savage sport. Men fought with bare knuckles. There were no rounds. And bouts went on until one man fell.

Another problem at that time was that fans would sometimes jump into the ring and enter into the fighting. To prevent this, the ring was raised six feet off the ground—where it remains today.

Not until 1867 did modern boxing come into being. At that time a man named Queensberry laid down the basic rules of boxing that we follow today. The rules said that the fighters would wear padded gloves. They said that there would be three-minute rounds with one-minute rest periods in between. And they said that a man who was down could not be hit.

Modern boxing has been around a little more than a century. During that time there have been some very strange fights.

One of these was a match between Andy Bowen and Jack Burke. The fight went on for 110 rounds! After more than seven hours, both fighters gave up and the bout was called a "no contest."

The Bowen-Burke fight was the longest ever. The shortest was between Al Couture and Ralph Walton. Walton was knocked out ½ second after the fight started!

Last but not least was a match between Primo Carnera and Tommy Loughran. Carnera weighed 270 pounds; Loughran, only 184! We wish we could end on a happy note and say that "little" Loughran won—but he didn't.

GOLF

The word "golf" comes from the Dutch word *kolf,* meaning "club." The ancient Romans, Dutch, and Scots all played forms of the game.

The first golf club was a stick with a bent end. In time, separate wooden heads were bound to the sticks. Later, iron heads were used in place of the wooden ones.

The first golf ball was made of solid wood. Later, the *featherie* was invented. The featherie consisted of a little leather cover stuffed with boiled goose feathers. To make it hard, a volume of feathers which would fill a beaver hat was stuffed into the tiny cover.

In 1848 a ball was invented that was made of solid gutta-percha, a very hard type of rubber. After a while it was found that an old, nicked-up ball was better than a new, smooth one. Instead of waiting for a ball to get bashed up, golfers began cutting little nicks all over it. In time, golf-ball manufacturers began molding balls with a pattern of little dimples.

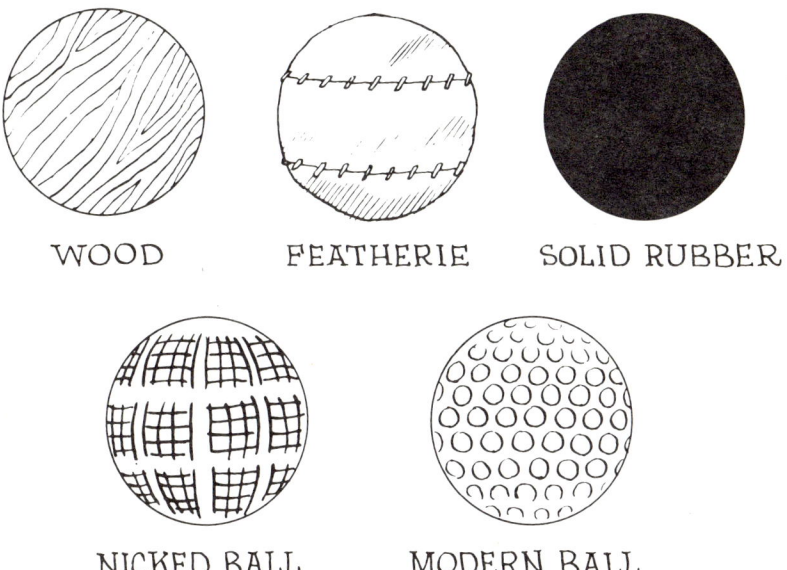

Solid rubber balls were used for about fifty years. Then, around 1900, rubber-core balls like those we use today were invented by Americans.

The first golf courses were just grass-covered meadows. The number of "holes" depended upon the amount of good land available. Sometimes the golfers played two or three holes. Sometimes they played twenty.

The eighteen-hole course became the fashion in 1764. In that year it was decided that a golf course should be nine holes—played "out" and "back." Later, instead of playing the same nine holes twice, nine more holes were added, which made the eighteen-hole course we still use today.

Like all sports, golf has had its odd moments.

In 1949 Harry Bradshaw hit a ball that landed in a bottle. A golf ball cannot be moved. So on his next shot, Harry smashed the bottle with his club and sent the ball about thirty feet.

In 1912 a woman golfer hit her ball into a river. The ball floated downstream. After chasing it more than a mile in a rowboat, she finally caught up with the ball. One hundred and sixteen strokes later, she finally putted the ball into the cup.

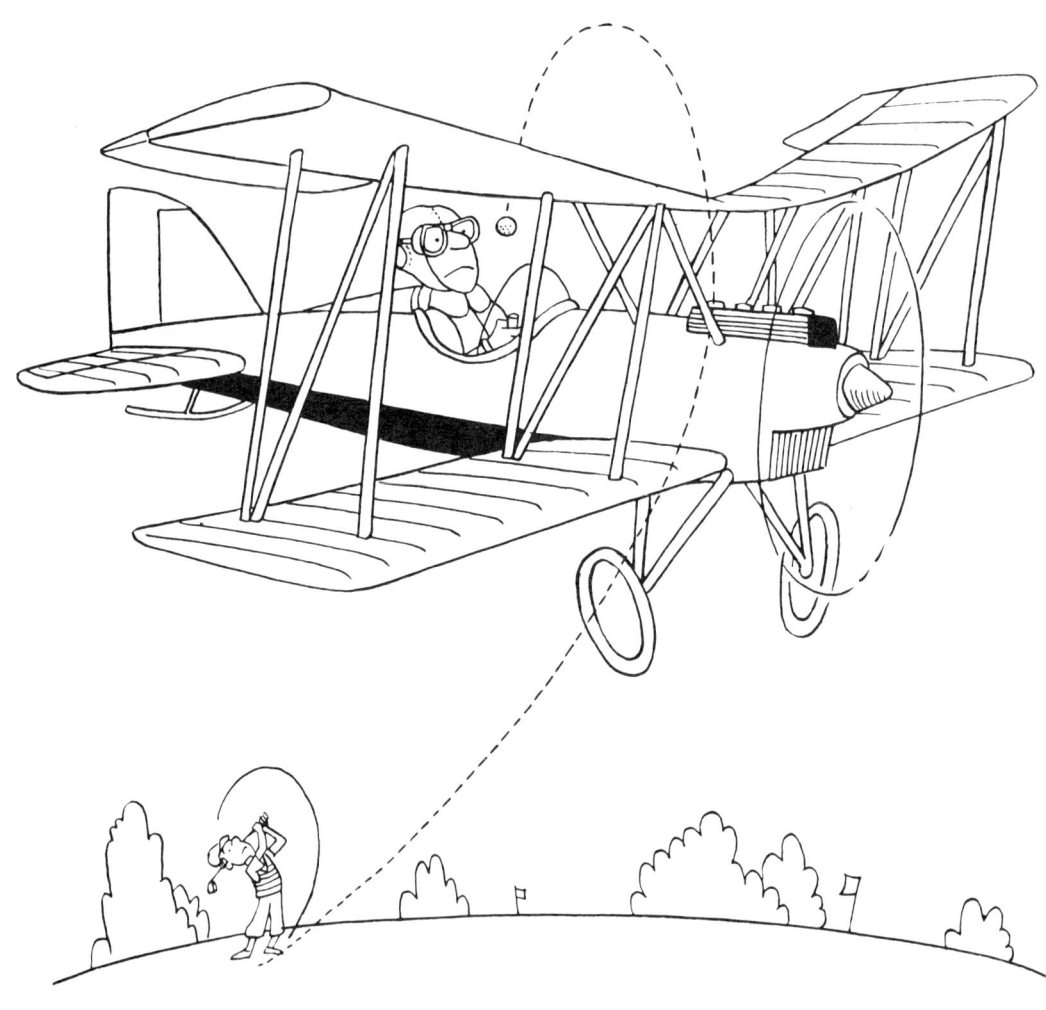

    Of all the things that have ever happened in golf, the strangest was the day a man hit a ball ninety miles! In 1929 a golfer in Texas hit a high drive. His ball fell into an airplane. An hour or two later it landed at the airport, ninety miles away.

BASEBALL

In the early days of baseball there were no bases. Instead, wooden stakes were used to show the runner's path. In the very beginning there was only one stake. A score was made when the batter ran to the stake and back to home plate.

In those days the fielders were allowed to throw the ball at the runner to make an out. This was called "plugging."

Over the years, more stakes were added. But the stakes were dangerous, so the players began using flat rocks or sandbags as bases.

At that time there were four bases instead of three. The runner scored by reaching fourth base. He did not have to return home to score.

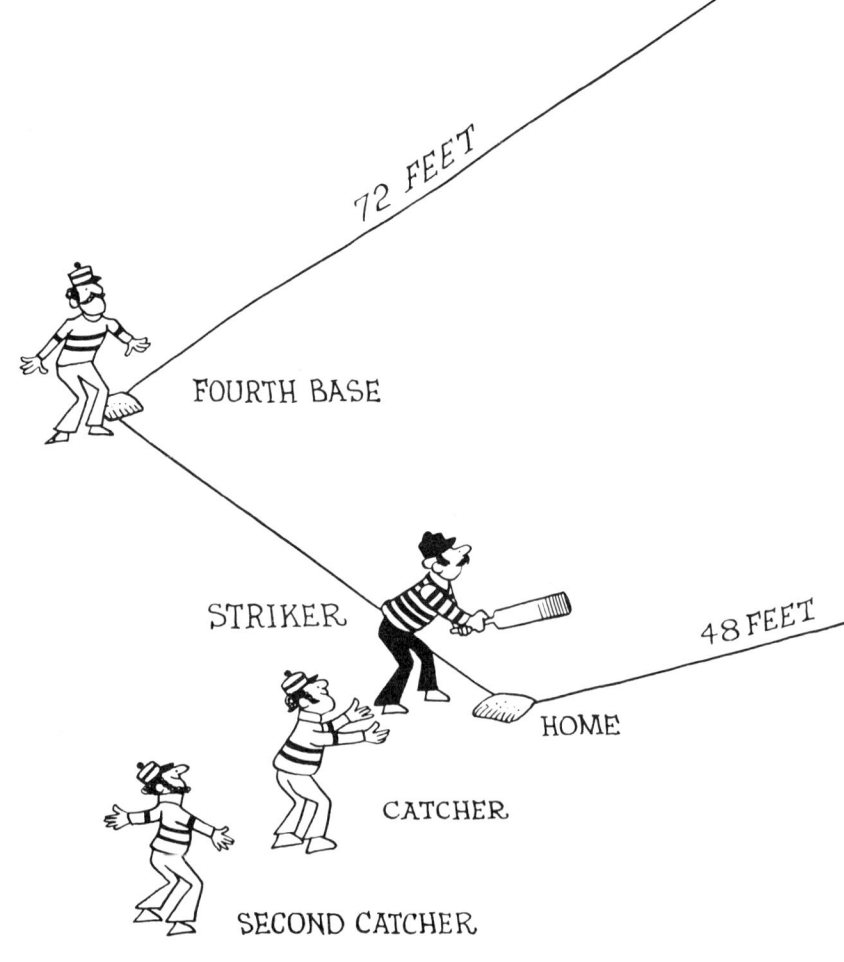

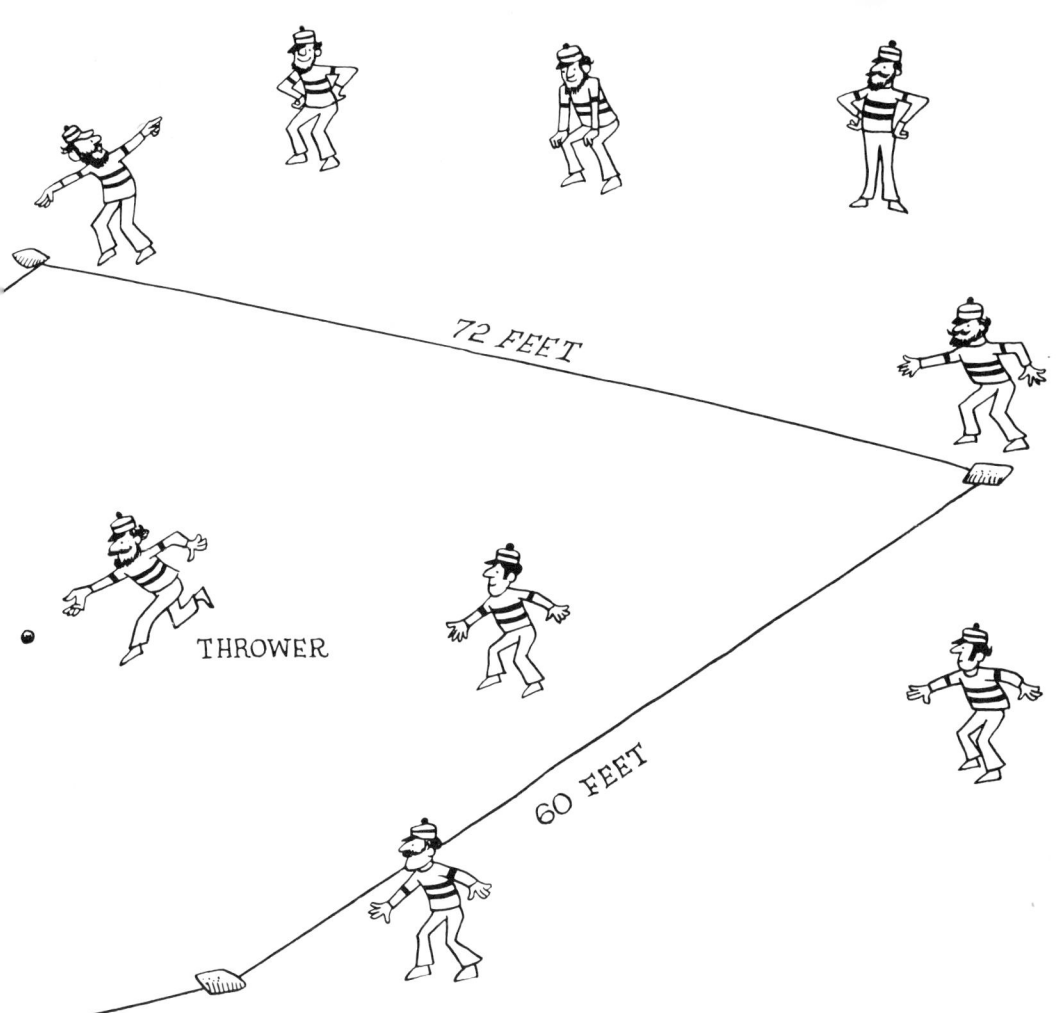

Teams of twelve played this early type of baseball. The pitcher was called a "thrower," and the batter was called a "striker." There were two catchers, one behind the other.

Runs were then called "aces." Instead of playing by innings, the first team to get twenty-one "aces" was the winner.

In the middle of the last century a man named Alexander Cartwright really got the game of baseball started. He changed the base setup from the four-base square to the diamond we use now. He set up a code of rules. And he arranged the first game on record.

But baseball still had a long way to go before it became the game of today. In Cartwright's time the players wore straw hats, flannel shirts, and wool pants. None of the players wore gloves. A ball caught on one bounce was an out. And it took four strikes instead of three to make an out.

The type of baseball that people were playing in Cartwright's time sounds pretty strange to us today. But who knows? Maybe the game we play today will seem just as odd to the people of the future.

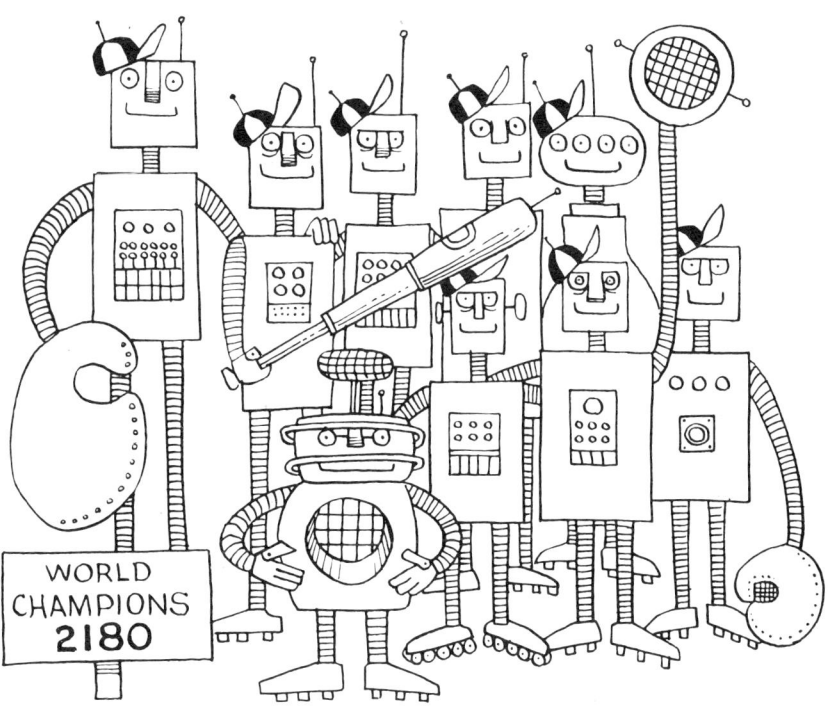

In two or three hundred years there may be all sorts of rule changes. Will two strikes be an out? Will there be ten bases instead of three? And what about the players? Will they still be human? Or is it possible that they will be machines?

This illustration of a skier is based on a rock carving dating from 2,000 B.C.

SKIING

Skiing began in northern Europe and Asia long before the dawn of history. Pictures and carvings of skiers done by Stone Age people have been found in Russia and other places. Even more interesting, a perfectly preserved ski was found in a bog in Norway. After examining it, scientists concluded that the ski was close to 5,000 years old!

Hunters on skis, from a map printed in 1539.

The word *ski*, which comes from northern Europe, means "a splinter cut from a log." Pronounced "shee," it is the Scandinavian term for shoe.

According to experts, the first skis were probably made from the bones of large animals. Later came wooden skis made from slabs of pine, spruce, or ash. To make them slide better over the surface of the snow, some early skis were covered with skin from elk, reindeer, or seal. Other skis had wooden strips or runners along the bottom.

Usually the ski was strapped to the foot with leather thongs or a leather harness. A few early skis had a footrest carved into the surface of the wood.

It took a long time for skis to become standardized. In fact, in the eleventh century many persons wore a different-length ski on each foot! On the right foot they wore a short, "kicking" ski, and on the left a longer, "running" ski.

Early skiers used only one ski pole, not two. The pole, which consisted of a heavy branch, was held between the skis for steering and balance. Later, bone points were attached to the end and a hoop to its top. Not until 1615 did skiers begin to use two poles, as we do today.

The earliest recorded skiing in the United States took place in California in 1856. In that year John "Snowshoe" Thompson, a Norwegian by birth, carried the mail to miners in the high Sierras, traveling on skis much of the time. Soon the miners themselves began skiing. Eager for excitement, they took to racing down the steep mountains.

Strangely, it was an Englishman who introduced skiing to the Alpine countries of Europe. In 1888 a Colonel Napier brought skis to Switzerland, and was looked upon as a madman by the natives. The following year Napier returned with Arthur Conan Doyle, the famous creator of Sherlock Holmes. Little by little, skiing began to gain in favor with the people of the region.

The first recorded use of skis in war was in A.D. 1200. In that year King Sverre of Sweden equipped his reconnaissance troops with skis. By the sixteenth century entire armies were going into battle on skis.

By World War II (1939–1945) skiing had become an established part of modern warfare.

Surprisingly, not until the nineteenth century did people begin to think of skiing as a sport. In 1767, as part of a military exercise, Norwegian soldiers competed by racing down steep slopes "without riding or leaning on their sticks." The first ski jump took place at Huseby Hill, near Oslo, Norway, in 1879.

Today skiing is practiced throughout the world—even in such unlikely places as Morocco, Hawaii, Lebanon, and Korea. In the United States alone there are more than 500 ski hills, some as far south of the Mason-Dixon line as North Carolina and Tennessee. Even in places where there is no snow, people have found a way to ski—they just make their own.

BADMINTON

The game of badminton was originally called shuttlecock. The name was changed to badminton around 1870.

At that time there lived an English duke who loved sports, especially "the game of shuttlecocks." Almost every weekend the duke invited his friends over to play the game at his home. The duke's home was a mansion—a mansion called Badminton. Little by little the game took on the name of the place where it was such a popular pastime.

BADMINTON

The duke did not invent badminton. He only gave it its name. To understand how the sport actually began, we have to go back many centuries to the time of the ancient Babylonians.

The Babylonians were a very superstitious people. They engaged in many magic rites which they thought would reveal the future. Among these rites was one in which two people hit a ball or other object back and forth. The length of time the ball could be kept in play supposedly revealed how long the people would live.

Little by little this magic rite turned into nothing more than a game. Sometimes the game was played by just one person. Here the object was to hit the shuttlecock into the air as many times as possible without letting it drop to the ground.

In another early version of the game the object was for the players to protect a target. Both players had to stand in one place. Then they took turns hitting the shuttle at the target behind their opponent.

Originally, the shuttlecock was a round piece of cork with goose feathers stuck around its top. Early shuttles varied greatly in size, weight, and design.

At first, people used the outstretched palm as a racket. The palm was replaced by a small bat of solid wood. Eventually, a frame with strings stretched across it came into use.

Around the turn of the century the idea of using a net came into being. At the same time, boundary markers were set up and rules of the game were established.

Americans did not take to the sport until the end of World War I. At that time, American soldiers were returning home from Europe. Some had been in England, where they had learned an interesting new sport called badminton. Once they were back home, their enthusiasm for the sport quickly spread to others.

Today, badminton is an international sport. Since 1948, annual tournaments have been held to determine the world champion. The sport is one that can be enjoyed by everyone—children and adults, carefree amateurs and highly skilled pros.

Don L. Wulffson teaches English, creative writing, and remedial reading at San Fernando High School in California. He also writes educational books, stories, poems, learning activities, and articles on education. Almost everything he writes for publication he uses in his classroom. "I wrote one sports history for my students, and because the kids liked it so much I wrote *How Sports Came To Be*," he says. A graduate of U.C.L.A., he is the recipient of the Distinguished Achievement Award for Excellence in Educational Journalism given by the Educational Press Association of America (1978). With his wife and two daughters, he lives in Northridge, California.

Roy Doty is a distinguished illustrator whose work has received many honors. He is the winner of two art director awards, and has been voted Cartoonist Illustrator of the Year three times by the National Cartoonists Society. An author as well as an illustrator, he has one book in Lothrop's Fun-To-Read series: *Old One-Eye Meets His Match*. A graduate of the Columbus School of Art in Columbus, Ohio, he has been a free-lance artist in the New York area since 1946. With his wife and two of his four children, he lives in West Redding, Connecticut.